The Door in the Wall

Marguerite De Angeli

TEACHER GUIDE

NOTE:

The trade book edition of the novel used to prepare this guide is found in the Novel Units catalog and on the Novel Units website. Using other editions may have varied page references.

Please note: We have assigned Interest Levels based on our knowledge of the themes and ideas of the books included in the Novel Units sets, however, please assess the appropriateness of this novel or trade book for the age level and maturity of your students prior to reading with them. You know your students best!

ISBN 978-1-56137-288-1

To order, contact your local school supply store, or:

Toll-Free Fax: 877.716.7272
Phone: 888.650.4224
3901 Union Blvd., Suite 155
St. Louis, MO 63115

sales@novelunits.com

novelunits.com

Table of Contents

Summary 3

Pre-reading Information and Activities 4

Ten Chapters...9

   Chapters contain: Vocabulary Words
   and Activities, Discussion Questions,
   Predictions, Supplementary Activities

Post-reading Questions 24

Post-reading Activities...25

Assessment..29

Skills and Strategies

Thinking
   Brainstorming, classifying
   and categorizing, evaluating,
   analyzing details

Comprehension
   Predicting, sequencing,
   decision-making, using
   reference materials,
   inference

Vocabulary
   Antonyms/synonyms, word
   maps, context

Writing
   Narrative, schedule, chart-
   report, chapter titles, letter,
   dialogue, descriptive

Listening/Speaking
   Participation in discussions,
   participation in dramatic
   activities

Literary Elements
   Character, setting, plot
   development, symbol

Summary

In this 1949 Newbery Medal winner, 10-year-old Robin is separated from his parents for several months. During this time, he does a lot of growing up as he copes with a new handicap, suffers physical and emotional hardship, and risks death to save his people from the enemy.

Robin's father goes off to the Scottish wars and his mother leaves to be the Queen's lady-in-waiting. Dame Ellen is supposed to care for Robin until John-the-Fletcher arrives, but the plan falls apart unbeknownst to Robin's parents.

Robin falls ill and Dame Ellen faithfully tends him for awhile despite his peevishness; fortunately it is not the deadly plague which afflicts many around him, but unfortunately Dame Ellen is soon stricken, herself. Brother Luke, a kind wandering friar, hears that Dame Ellen has been taken of the plague, and goes to Robin. Since Robin can no longer walk, Brother Luke plants him on a horse and supports him during the ride to St. Mark's. A few months later finds Robin quite settled in the monastery routine. He enjoys listening to the chanting of the monks and watching the visiting pilgrims, knights, merchants, and minstrels. One day Brother Luke sets up a bench and brings Robin a knife and piece of pine for whittling. When the little boat is finished, Brother Luke brings him some pieces of walnut and suggests making a cross. Then he takes Robin to the scriptorium, where records, poems, and psalteries are copied and promises to teach Robin to read and write. Stopping at the chapel on the way back, Robin and Brother Luke meet a cheerful, lame boy maneuvering easily on crutches who greets Robin as "Brother Crookshanks"—to Robin's consternation. Brother Luke scolds the boy, Geoffrey Atte-Water, saying that Robin's legs will one day be as good as his. Spring comes, and Brother Luke takes Robin to the garden, where Brother Matthew shows him how to use some better cutting tools. Unfortunately, the chisel slips and breaks the cross, bringing an angry outburst from Robin. Seeing the boy's frustration, Brother Luke explains that they shall divide the days into teaching Robin's mind and teaching his hands, so that he will be occupied, and not get so easily discouraged.

Summer comes and Robin whittles a small doll for a poor little girl who has been hanging onto him. On an outing with Brother Luke one day, Robin sees Geoffrey swimming, and agrees with Brother Luke that he can learn to swim, which he does daily from that point on—rain or shine. He makes friends with the boys, whittling a boat for each, and playing outdoor games with them. After much careful work, he makes himself some crutches and learns to use them. A messenger, John-go-in-the-Wynd comes with a letter from Robin's father, who asks that Brother Luke and John accompany Robin on a journey to Shropshire. Preparations are made and the three set out, sharing one horse between them, only to get lost on their way to the White Swan. To Robin's great joy, they consequently sleep under the stars. The next night brings worse calamity; they stop at a run-down inn where thieves plot to steal their possessions. Luckily Robin overhears them, and wakes the others, who escape out the back window in the nick of time with the would-be-robbers in hot pursuit.

The fourth day finds them at Oxford, surrounded by poor students in multicolored gowns, where they spend the night. The next day they stop at a fair, where Robin is delighted by the food, tournaments, wrestling, bear-baiting, and Punch and Judy (puppet) show—and spend the night at an abbey. The next night they are welcomed into the cottage of a woodman, grateful to John for the help the latter had previously rendered when the woodcutter once injured himself.

Finally they arrive at the Castle Lindsay where they are welcomed by Sir Peter, whom Robin is supposed to serve as page. John stays for a time while Robin finds his way about and learns his routine (helping the boys cut their meat, learning to use the bow-and-arrow, etc.). Robin makes a new friend—D'Ath, the hound, and begins making a wooden harp, with John's help. November arrives and John decides it is time to leave to pay a visit to his mother, first describing the route to Robin. Meanwhile, those in the castle grow increasingly ill at ease; the Welsh are threatening to attack. Indeed, word comes that the Welsh are hammering at the town gate and have killed the watchman. The town is taken; fog enshrouds the castle; Robin learns patience as he works on his harp; food and water dwindle.

Finally Robin decides to embark on a bold mission. Telling only Brother Luke and a fellow page, Robin slips out before dawn to seek help from Sir Fitzhugh. He is almost captured by a Welsh guard, who luckily mistakes him for a poor shepherd. Finally Robin finds the house of John-go-in-the-Wynd's mother; John and Robin enter the town through a shoemaker's house, after John gives the secret harp-tune signal. Passing through the shoemaker's garden, they make their way to the church, where they wait an hour, then sound the alarm by ringing the great bell. Sir Hugh's men enter, take the town from the Welsh, and march the invaders out of town.

Sir Peter praises Robin and rewards John with a holding of land and portion of sheep. The days pass, winter comes, and preparations are made for Christmas. Then, at last, the King and his company arrive—including Robin's mother and father! There is a happy reunion, after which Robin is summoned before the King, who presents "Sir Robin" with a jeweled collar in token of his grateful thanks for Robin's brave actions. In return, Robin gets out his harp and offers a song of Christmas. In response to Robin's anxious question, his parents tell him that they don't care about his misshapen legs, but are just happy that all can return home to London together—with Brother Luke as Robin's tutor—after the Feast of Christmas.

Prior to Reading

You may wish to choose one or more of the following prereading discussion questions/activities. Each is designed to help students draw from their store of background knowledge about the events and themes they will meet in the story they are about to read.

Pre-reading Discussion Questions

You may elicit or provide the following background information:

On The Middle Ages: Why was the Middle Ages also known as the "Dark Ages"? Who was Charlemagne? Do you think he should have been called Charles the Great? Why or why not? What were "pilgrimages"? What did people wear? eat? play?

On Being Disabled: What problems would you have if you lost the use of your legs? How would your difficulties be different from those of someone who had never been able to walk? How could you compensate in today's world? Without all the high-tech devices available in today's world, how would a person compensate for the loss of use of his or her legs?

On Courage: What is courage? Why do people do brave things? What is the most courageous thing you have ever done?

Pre-reading Activities

The period between about 400 AD-1350 is referred to as the "Middle Ages." This is the period during which the story you are about to read takes place. Think about what it was like to live in England during that time period. Then look at the list below. Mark those items which WERE around during the Middle Ages "Y" and mark those which were NOT around yet "N." (As you read the story, see if any of your answers would change.)

_____ hide and seek	_____ harps
_____ Monopoly	_____ electric guitars
_____ hot dogs	_____ flu shots
_____ pudding	_____ curfews
_____ popcorn	_____ newspapers
_____ pet dogs	_____ telephones
_____ Christmas carols	_____ churches
_____ ballads	_____ bathing suits
_____ rhythm and blues	_____ crutches
_____ country fairs	_____ wheelchairs

Filmstrip

View a filmstrip on feudalism. During the filmstrip, stop three times to ask: 1) Compare how fairy tales show kings with how the film shows nobles and kings. 2) Compare how fairy tales, cartoons, stories, etc. show knights with how the film shows them. 3) Contrast the lives of the peasants, the middle class, and the lords and nobles.

Role Play

Monks like the ones you are about to meet in the story often had to spend long periods of silence. Spend a day keeping a vow of silence (dressed, perhaps in a "monk's habit"—choir robe). Afterward, discuss what you thought of "being" a monk. What was good about it? What didn't you like?

Recommended Procedure for Reading this Book

This book will be read one section at a time, using DRTA (Directed Reading Thinking Activity) Method. This technique involves reading a section and predicting what will happen next (making good guesses) based on what has already occurred in the story. The students continue to read and everyone verifies the predictions.

Bulletin Board or Worksheet Idea: Semantic Mapping

1. Write the phrase MIDDLE AGES on a large sheet of paper taped to the board. Have students brainstorm words, phrases, and general information they associate with the Middle Ages. List the words on the board, then organize them into clusters with student help. Tell students they will be viewing a movie or filmstrip about the Middle Ages, and should watch for both information to add to the categories they created, as well as new categories they missed. (See the sample map below.)

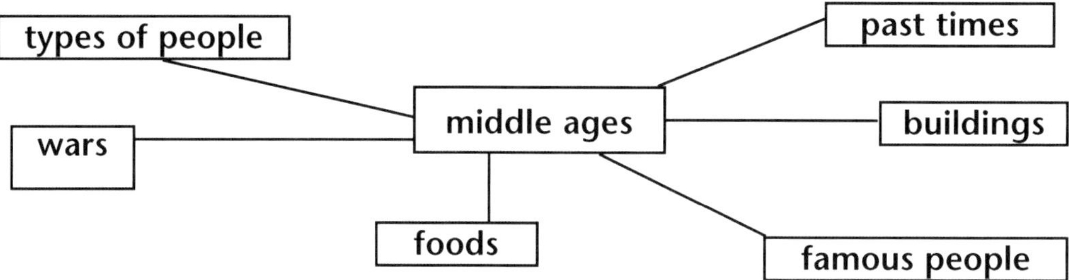

2. Then, after viewing a movie (such as "Medieval England, the Peasants Revolt" or "The Middle Ages: A Wanderers Guide to Life and Letters"—available through many media centers), have students suggest additions to the map. Finally, explain that *The Door in the Wall* is set in the Middle Ages, and that students will be adding to the map as they read.

3. Post the map on the bulletin board and have student volunteers decorate it with representations we associate with medieval times, such as medieval dresses, armor, castles, etc.

Setting the Purpose: Initiating Activity

After looking at the cover and flipping through the illustrations inside the book, what do you predict the story will be about? Where will it take place? When? What is the purpose of a "door in the wall"? What can you tell about the three people in the picture? What do you suppose brought them together? Where do you think they are going? Read *The Door in the Wall* to find out about the problems—some annoying, some funny, some life-threatening—faced by the boy on the cover.

Using Predictions

We all make predictions as we read—little guesses about what will happen next, how a conflict will be resolved, which details will be important to the plot, which details will help fill in our sense of a character. Students should be encouraged to predict, to make sensible guesses as they read the novel.

As students work on their predictions, these discussion questions can be used to guide them: What are some of the ways to predict? What is the process of a sophisticated reader's thinking and predicting? What clues does an author give to help us make predictions? Why are some predictions more likely to be accurate than others?

Create a chart for recording predictions. This could be either an individual or class activity. As each subsequent chapter is discussed, students can review and correct their previous predictions about plot and characters as necessary.

Use the facts and ideas the author gives.

Use your own prior knowledge.

Apply any new information (i.e., from class discussion) that may cause you to change your mind.

Predictions:

Prediction Chart

What characters have we met so far?	What is the conflict in the story?	What are your predictions?	Why did you make those predictions?

Chapter 1, Pages 7-17

Vocabulary

coverlet (7)	Nones (7)	clamoring (7)	vexation (7)
gentil (7)	liege (7)	mailed (7)	solar (8)
plague (8)	fletcher (8)	joust (9)	shire reeve (9)
putrid (9)	coif (9)	Cockney (9)	Norman (10)
wheedling (10)	victuals (11)	grotesque (11)	bosses (11)
corbels (11)	embrasure (11)	carters (11)	retainer (12)
Vespers (12)	friar (12)	hospice (12)	cloisters (15)
pallets (15)	woefully (15)	tethered (16)	jennet (16)
dost (16)	hosen (16)	frock (16)	sedately (17)
curfew (17)	habit (17)	postern (17)	

Vocabulary Activity

Working alone or with a partner, decide on four categories into which the target vocabulary words can be divided. Place each word under one of the headings. Guess if you do not know a word's meaning, then see if your guesses change as you read the story.

Discussion Questions

1. What is shown in the picture on page 6? What happens in the next few days following what is shown? *(Robin is saying good-bye to his mother, who is going to serve the queen; the next day he grows ill and can't use his legs.)*

2. What is Robin like? How do you know? Begin the attribute web on the next page. *(He is a 10-year-old boy; comes from a noble family; tries to be brave; expects to learn the ways of knighthood; cannot use his legs because of illness; and can be arrogant and rude.)*

3. Where is Robin's father? How did Robin feel when his father left? *(Robin's father has gone to lead soldiers in the Scottish wars; Robin felt sad when his father left, but proud of his father.)*

4. How does Dame Ellen treat Robin? Why? How does he treat her? Why? What does this show you about both of them? *(She kindly tries to get him to eat, even though she doesn't feel well herself; he throws the porridge at her. She is loyal and self-sacrificing; he is angry about his powerlessness, and acts somewhat like a spoiled brat.)*

5. Would Dame Ellen have returned if Robin had been nicer to her? How do you know? *(Probably not; even though she is angry with him, the main reason she doesn't return, Brother Luke reveals, is that she has been stricken by plague.)*

6. What was the plan Robin's parents had made for Robin? How and why does the plan change? *(He was supposed to be taken by John-the-Fletcher to Sir Peter de Lindsay, where he would learn to be a knight; because Robin falls ill and John does not come, Robin goes instead to a monastery with Brother Luke.)*

Attribute Web

The attribute web below will help you gather clues the author provides about a character in the novel. Fill in the blanks with words and phrases which tell how the character acts and looks, as well as what the character says and what others say about him or her.

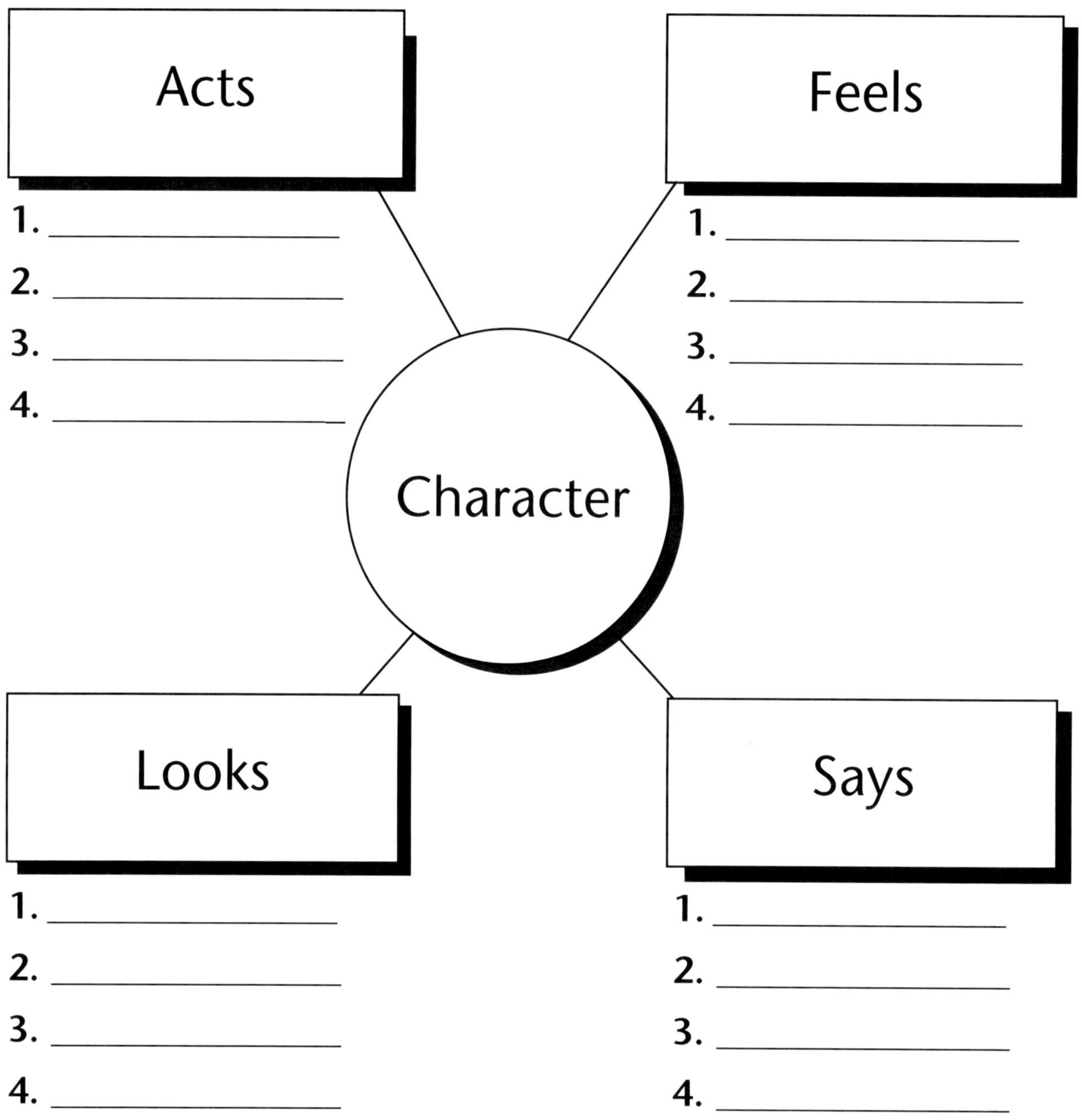

7. What problem does Brother Luke face in getting Robin to St. Mark's? How does he solve the problem? What else could he have done? *(He carries Robin on his back to the horse, straps Robin on the horse and walks alongside, supporting the boy.)*

8. How does Robin feel when they reach St. Mark's? Why doesn't Brother Luke send a messenger right away to Robin's father? *(He is fearful and wants to know when he will go home; Brother Luke plans to send the messenger when the plague is somewhat quieted—perhaps because he doesn't want Robin's father to be exposed to plague, and also because everyone is so busy right now caring for the sick.)*

Prediction

How long do you think it will be before Robin sees his parents again? What will life at the monastery be like for him?

Literary Analysis Symbol

A symbol is something that stands for something else. For example, a heart might stand for love, or a flag might stand for a country. Symbols often appear in stories. When an object or phrase is repeated several times throughout a story, you should ask yourself whether that object or word stands for something else. Repetition is a clue to symbolism.

Brother Luke uses the phrase "the door in the wall."

a) Where have you already seen this phrase? *(the title)*

b) Where is the door in the wall Brother Luke describes? *(He is describing the route they will take to the monastery; they go out through the door in the wall of the courtyard, into the street, and in the door at the gate to St. Mark's.)*

c) What other kind of door is Brother Luke talking about? What does he really mean? *(He is telling Robin to be hopeful; no matter how difficult problems may seem, there is always a solution if you have patience and keep looking for it.)*

d) Begin a list of all pages on which you find the phrase repeated; in each case, jot down how the phrase "door in the wall" is used and what it means.

Chapter 2, Pages 18-25

Vocabulary

hawthorn (18)	clamored (18)	procession (18)	devotions (18)
breviary (18)	pilgrims (19)	minstrels (19)	almonry (19)
whittle (20)	mutton (20)	seethed (20)	awry (21)
bowsprit (21)	pennant (21)	retainers (22)	weathered (22)
keepsake (22)	proportioned (22)	pumice (23)	criptorium (23)
psalteries (23)	parchment (23)	illumined (23)	crookshank (24)
impertinent (24)	conduit (24)		

Vocabulary Activity

Many of the words in the story would be familiar to someone living in the Middle Ages, but seem unusual to modern-day readers.

Working by yourself or with a partner, guess in which category each of the underlined vocabulary words belongs. Label the word "I" if you think you would find it inside of a monastery. Label the word "O" if you think you would find it outside the monastery. Put both letters, if found in both places. See if any of your labels change as you read the story.

Discussion Questions

1. How much time has passed since Robin grew ill? *(a few months; March—May)*

2. What were some of the types of people in the monastery? Why were there so many people there? *(Some were ill, others were poor and in need of food and clothing, others—visiting pilgrims, knights, merchants, minstrels—stopped in their travels because there were few inns.)*

3. What does Brother Luke teach Robin? Why? *(He teaches Robin how to smooth the wood on the boat he is making; he also promises to teach him to read and write so that he will have less time to feel depressed.)*

4. Why is the boat more special to Robin than other toys he has had? Have you ever felt this way about something you made? *(He made the boat, whereas the other toys were made for him.)*

5. How did Robin become interested in learning to write? *(He was shown the manuscripts on which the monks worked, and wished he could read the records, poems, psalteries, etc.)*

6. Why is Robin angry with Geoffrey Atte-Water? Would you be? *(The boy kiddingly refers to Robin's lameness, by calling him "Brother Crookshanks.")*

7. How does Robin feel as he goes into the chapel? Why? How do his feelings change? *(He feels angry, and worries about how his father will react to his disability; as he begins his prayers, he feels better.)*

Prediction

How will Robin's father react to his son's disability?

Writing Activity

Write about a time when you, like Robin, had to restrict your activity because of an injury or illness. What did you do with your time? Who helped you? How did you feel?

Chapter 3, Pages 26-31

Vocabulary

abated (26)	refectory (26)	chapel (26)	trundle cart (26)
chisel (27)	tonsured (31)	minced words (31)	

Vocabulary Activity

Answer the following questions.

1. When a snowstorm abates, what does it do?

2. What would you find in a refectory?

3. What would you do in a chapel?

4. How is a trundle cart different from a wheelbarrow?

5. What might you use a chisel for?

6. How is a tonsured head different from a bald one?

7. How can you tell your parents you flunked a test, without mincing words?

Discussion Questions

1. Where does Brother Luke carry Robin? Why? *(He takes him to the garden so that he can whittle in the fresh air and learn from Brother Matthew.)*

2. Why did Robin get angry and hurl his chisel? *(The tool slipped and the cross broke.)* What do you think would have been a better way to handle his anger? (Complete the exercise on the following activity page.)

3. How can you tell Brother Matthew has a sense of humor? *(He promises not to tell Brother Luke how he nearly lost his head.)*

4. What does Brother Luke mean when he says that "reading is another door in the wall"? *(Reading is another way to escape your worries, and learn how to solve your problems.)*

5. How do Robin's reading/writing lessons begin? How is this similar to/different from the way you learned to read and write? How would you teach a 10-year-old to write? *(He writes a letter dictated by Robin and then reads the letter back, pointing out each letter and word.)*

6. Why does Brother Luke say to Robin, "Thou hast not minced words in thy letter"? What tone of voice do you think he uses? *(Robin is very direct about what has happened to him—how close he came to death, how useless his legs are, and how anxious he is to get a letter.)*

Prediction

When will Robin's father answer? What will he say?

Writing Activities

1. Write about a time when reading was a "door in the wall" for you.

2. Write out Robin's daily schedule.

Activity Sheet: Decision-Making

Directions:

    a)   Brainstorm a list of things you can do when you are angry.

    b)   Think of advantages and disadvantages of each.

    c)   Circle those things Robin could have done when he accidentally broke the cross.

    d)   Put a star by the reaction you think would have been best.

    e)   Explain why this would have been the best way for him to react.

Reactions	Pros	Cons

My choice for the best reaction: _______________________

Why I made this choice: _____________________________________

Chapter 4, Pages 32-41

Vocabulary

hovel (32)	crusaders (35)	droned (36)	fasting (36)
jerkin (37)	habit (37)	hosen (37)	lectern (38)
missal (38)	chantry (38)	weir (39)	fervently (40)
guild (41)			

Vocabulary Activity

Circle the word in each group of words that LEAST belongs with the others. Write a sentence or two explaining why the word does not belong.

1. guild association minstrel club
   (minstrel; Minstrels are wandering singers—the rest are all organizations.)

2. weir chantry fence net dam
   (chantry; Chantry is a chapel for singing and minor services—the others are synonyms.)

3. drone fast clatter peal
   (fast; Fasting is not eating—the others are sounds.)

4. habits jerkins crusaders hosen
   (crusaders; Crusaders were Christians trying to recover the Holy Land from the Muslims—the rest are clothes)

5. castle monastery hovel missal
   (missal; A missal is a prayer book—the rest are buildings.)

Discussion Questions

1. How much time has passed since Robin became ill? *(several months; March-summer)*

2. What does he decide to carve? for whom? How is Robin changing? *(a doll for the poor girl who has been clinging to him; Brother Luke is teaching him to do for others.)*

3. How does Robin learn to swim? Why? *(Brother Luke supports him and tells him what to do; Brother Luke thinks it will be good to strengthen Robin's arms in preparation for crutches; Robin wants to swim like the other boys.)*

4. How does Robin feel about the prospect of crutches? Have you ever felt that way? *(He has mixed feelings; he wants to be able to get about as Geoffrey does, but he worries about his father's reaction and how he will ride horseback when he needs crutches.)*

5. What does Brother Luke mean when he says that even the crutches can be a "door in the wall"? *(They can be a partial solution to the problem of being lame, and can open up new options for Robin.)*

6. How does Robin share with the boys? How is his relationship with them changing? *(He helps each make a boat of his own; instead of feeling jealous and at odds with them, he plays with them.)*

7. What is Robin's secret? Why does he choose the time he does to reveal it? *(He can now bear some weight on his feet; he wants to show that he can lean on the bench to help make his own crutches.)*

8. What is the city like? How does Robin feel about being back in the city again? *(There is a lot of merriment—food, drink, decorations for Midsummer's Eve. Robin is happy to experience the excitement again, but doesn't want to see his empty home.)*

Prediction
When will Robin leave the monastery? With whom?

Research Activity
Research the organization and function of guilds. Make up a chart showing some of the different guilds and which craftsmen belonged to each. Give an oral "chart talk."

Chapter 5, Pages 42-52

Vocabulary

cassock (42)	cotta (42)	verger (42)	alternating (42)
saddler (46)	ironmonger (46)	quench (46)	pilgrimage (47)
refuge (47)	lay (47)	cutpurse (48)	roisterer (48)
crook (48)	cowl (50)	galled (51)	fuller (51)
crop (52)	brocaded (52)	punky (52)	tinder (52)

Vocabulary Activity
Match each of the following with what he does:

1. Verger   _____   a. caretaker of the church

2. Saddler   _____   b. person who cleanses/thickens cloth

3. Cutpurse   _____   c. noisy boisterous type

4. Roisterer   _____   d. pickpocket, thief

5. Fuller   _____   e. person who makes horse equipment

(answers: 1a, 2e, 3d, 4c, 5b)

Discussion Questions
1. How long has it been since Robin's arrival at the monastery? *(about five months)*

2. How does Robin get a letter from his father? What effect does the letter have on his situation? *(John-go-in-the-Wynd, the minstrel, brings a message; Robin is to go to Shropshire with Brother Luke and John.)*

3. What plans are made for Robin's trip? How does he feel about leaving? Would you have taken anything else along? *(A sidesaddle is made, Robin's clothes are repaired, food is gathered, and a plan of travel is laid out; he is excited to be going, but sad to be leaving his friends.)*

4. Brother Luke compares the trip to a pilgrimage. How is the trip like a pilgrimage? *(p. 47, "for always we shall set forth for the honor of God and in the hope that young Robin will be even stronger at the end of our journey..."; A pilgrimage is a long journey made to a sacred place as an act of devotion.)*

5. Why does Robin decide he wants to make a harp? *(He admires John's harp-playing.)*

6. Why do Robin and the two adults sleep outside instead of at an inn, the first night? How does Robin feel about it? Why don't they sleep in the woods? *(They cannot find the inn and want to avoid the possibility of beasts and highwaymen in the woods; Robin is thrilled to sleep under the stars.)*

Writing Activity
Write about a time when food tasted particularly good because of how hungry you were. Describe specific foods and tastes, as the author did on page 52.

Prediction
Where will the travelers spend the next night? What problems will they encounter?

Chapter 6, Pages 53-61

Vocabulary
noggins (56)   granary (61)

Vocabulary Activity
Answer the following questions.
    What would you probably find in a noggin? *(ale)*

    What would you probably find in a granary? *(grain—oats, corn)*

Discussion Questions
1. Why does Luke insist that Robin swim? Should he? What is the effect on Robin? *(Luke wants Robin to keep his strength up; Robin complains of the cold, but is later glad he swam.)*

2. Why is John hesitant about staying at the "White Hart"? Why do they go in? What alternatives did they have? *(He thinks the people inside look like "ruffians," but they see no other choice.)*

3. What would have happened if Robin had slept? *(The robbers would have stolen their property, and possibly harmed them.)*

4. How does Robin alert the others to danger? What else could he have done? *(He first drags himself to Luke and wakes the friar up; Luke slowly opens the door so that sleeping John rolls in.)*

5. How does Robin help his friends escape from their pursuers? *(He uses his crutches to trip the thieves.)*

Prediction

Will Robin and the others have any more trouble before they reach their goal?

Writing Activity

The harp music makes the trip seem shorter to Robin. Make a list of suggestions for making a long car-trip seem shorter.

Chapter 7, Pages 62-75

Vocabulary

particolored (62)	caparison (62)	lombards (63)	hospitality (64)
flagon (65)	serf (66)	ingrate (66)	pease porridge (66)
emissaries (68)	keep (71)	bannock (73)	newel (73)
Percheron (73)	fletcher (74)	yeoman (74)	

Vocabulary Activity

Match the vocabulary words with their definitions

1. _____ caparison   a. arrow-maker

2. _____ Lombard   b. oatmeal cake

3. _____ flagon   c. decorative horse covering

4. _____ serf   d. thick cereal or soup

5. _____ porridge   e. large drinking bottle

6. _____ bannock   f. member of Northern Italian tribe

7. _____ newel   g. lesser freeholder, below gentry

8. _____ fletcher   h. person attached to lord's land

9. _____ yeoman   i. pillar at top of winding stairs

(answers: 1c, 2f, 3e, 4h, 5d, 6b, 7i, 8a, 9g)

Discussion Questions

1. Where did Robin and the others spend the fourth night? How did Robin like the people there? *(They stayed at the University—Oxford; Robin felt that the students were being deliberately outlandish in their dress.)*

2. What is the fair like? How is it like a modern day fair? How is it different? Which activities would you have liked best?

Medieval Fair	Modern-Day Fair
1. bear baiting	
2.	
3.	

3. Where do the travelers spend the fifth night? *(at an abbey; the abbot is hospitable)*

4. Why are the travelers welcomed by the woodman? *(He is grateful to John, who came to his aid when he was wounded by an ax.)*

5. How does Robin feel as he nears his destination? Why? *(He begins to dread meeting Lord Peter because he worries that he will be a poor page, because of his disability.)*

6. What does Peter mean, "If we do what we are able, a door always opens to something else"? Do you agree? *(Make the most of what you have, and you will create new opportunities for yourself.)*

7. How does Robin's new routine differ from the one he had at the monastery? *(Now he spends part of each day studying Latin, learning to shoot a bow and arrow, listening to stories and ballads, swimming, and attending to the Lady and boys at dinner.)*

8. Who is D'Ath? *(a dog who becomes a special friend)*

Prediction

How will Robin end up in danger? Will he ever be able to ride a horse?

Art Activity

Based on the description of the castle, illustrate it (with markers, diorama, collage, or another medium of your choice).

Chapter 8, Pages 76-85

Vocabulary

flageolet (79)	largess (79)	farrier (79)	bailey (80)
portcullis (83)	flambeaux (84)	fripperies (84)	trestles (84)

Vocabulary Activity

French derivations—Several English words are actually borrowed from the French. Which of the words in the list above do you think have French derivations? How do the meanings in English compare with the original meanings in French?

(Answers: flageolet—small flute with four finger-holes, is from the French flajolet=flute; largess—bestowing of gifts, is from largesse=generosity; farrier—blacksmith, is related to the French ferrier=smith; flambeau—flaming torch, is from the French flambe=flame)

Discussion Questions

1. Brother Luke says, "It is better to have crooked legs than a crooked spirit." What does he mean? Do you agree? *(It is far worse to lose mental abilities or spiritual strength than it is to lose physical abilities.)*

2. What are some of the games the boys play? Who are some of Robin's new friends? Did ten-year-olds play much differently from the way they play today? *(hide and seek, target shooting, duck on a rock; Denis and Alan)*

3. How can you tell that Robin is getting less easily frustrated; that he likes to challenge himself? *(He wants to work on the harp because, as John says, "anyone can NOT do it.")*

4. Why does John leave? *(He goes to visit his mother.)*

5. Why are there so few at supper? Why are tensions mounting? *(The men are on guard; it is said that the Welsh will attack.)*

6. Once the Welsh start attacking, what is Robin's task? *(He is responsible for delivering the boys safely to the keep.)*

Prediction

Will Robin get his harp? How will he help protect the castle from the invaders?

Art Activity

Illustrate the view of the surrounding area from the watchtower. Put a star on John's mother's house.

Chapter 9, Pages 86-103

Vocabulary

catapulting (86)	garrison (87)	sally port (90)	benedicite (91)
lancers (99)	drovers (99)	cumber (99)	priory (100)
pikestaff (103)	windlass (103)		

Vocabulary Activity

Complete each sentence in a way that shows you understand the meaning of the underlined word.

1. We need food because the garrison ___________________________

2. The monk said, "Benedicite ___________________________

3. The company of lancers ___________________________

4. When you get to the priory ___________________________

5. The sentry's pikestaff ___________________________

6. You might use a windlass to ___________________________

Discussion Questions

1. How do people pass the time while waiting for the attack? What would you do? *(Women do spinning, weaving, embroidery; children play with soldiers, hobbyhorses, dolls; Robin tells stories, sings, works on his harp.)*

2. What hardships do the people in the castle face as time goes on? How is this like what still happens to civilians in war time, today? *(Supplies of food and water dwindle.)*

3. Why does Robin decide to leave the castle? Why does he plan to keep the trip secret from Sir Peter? Is that right? *(He plans to go seek help from Sir Fitzhugh, but doesn't want Sir Peter to know because he would forbid Robin—with his disability—to go.)*

4. What does Robin plan to take? Would you have taken anything else? *(a smock, rags for his legs, a hood, thongs for tying his crutches to his back)*

5. How does the friar react to the plan? Were you surprised? *(He doesn't try to discourage Robin, just encourages him and asks him if he is afraid.)*

6. What does Robin say to himself as he swims? Do you have any favorite thoughts which give you courage when you are afraid or frustrated? *(He tells himself, "Anyone could NOT do it.")*

7. How does the enemy guard treat Robin? Why? *(quite kindly; He thinks Robin is a poor shepherd boy who has fallen into the water.)*

8. How does Robin find John? Why? *(He remembers the description John gave of his mother's cottage; Robin needs John to ask Sir Hugh for help.)*

9. Why might Sir Hugh help? Why might he not? *(He might help because he doesn't want the Welsh to bother him and because he is related to Sir Peter, who is threatened; he might not, because he does not really get along with Sir Peter.)*

10. What is the plan for getting into the church? Why? *(They will creep along the river, enter John's friend, the shoemaker's house, go from there to the church, where they will sound the alarm which lets Sir Hugh's men know when to attack.)*

11. How do Robin and John get into the shoemaker's house? *(After giving the harp signal, they grab a rope the shoemaker winds out his window.)*

Prediction

How will Robin's parents react when they see him? What will they say? How much will his disability bother them?

Drama Activity

Prepare a Reader's Theatre performance of this chapter. Record on tape, complete with sound effects (such as the clumping of the guard's pikestaff and the secret signal which gets John and Robin into the shoemaker's).

Vocabulary

sacristan (104) belfry (105) turrets (105) deliverance (106)
routed (109) viol (111) banners (115) dais (118)
doublet (118) realm (119)

Vocabulary Activity

Complete a word map like the sample below for target vocabulary words.

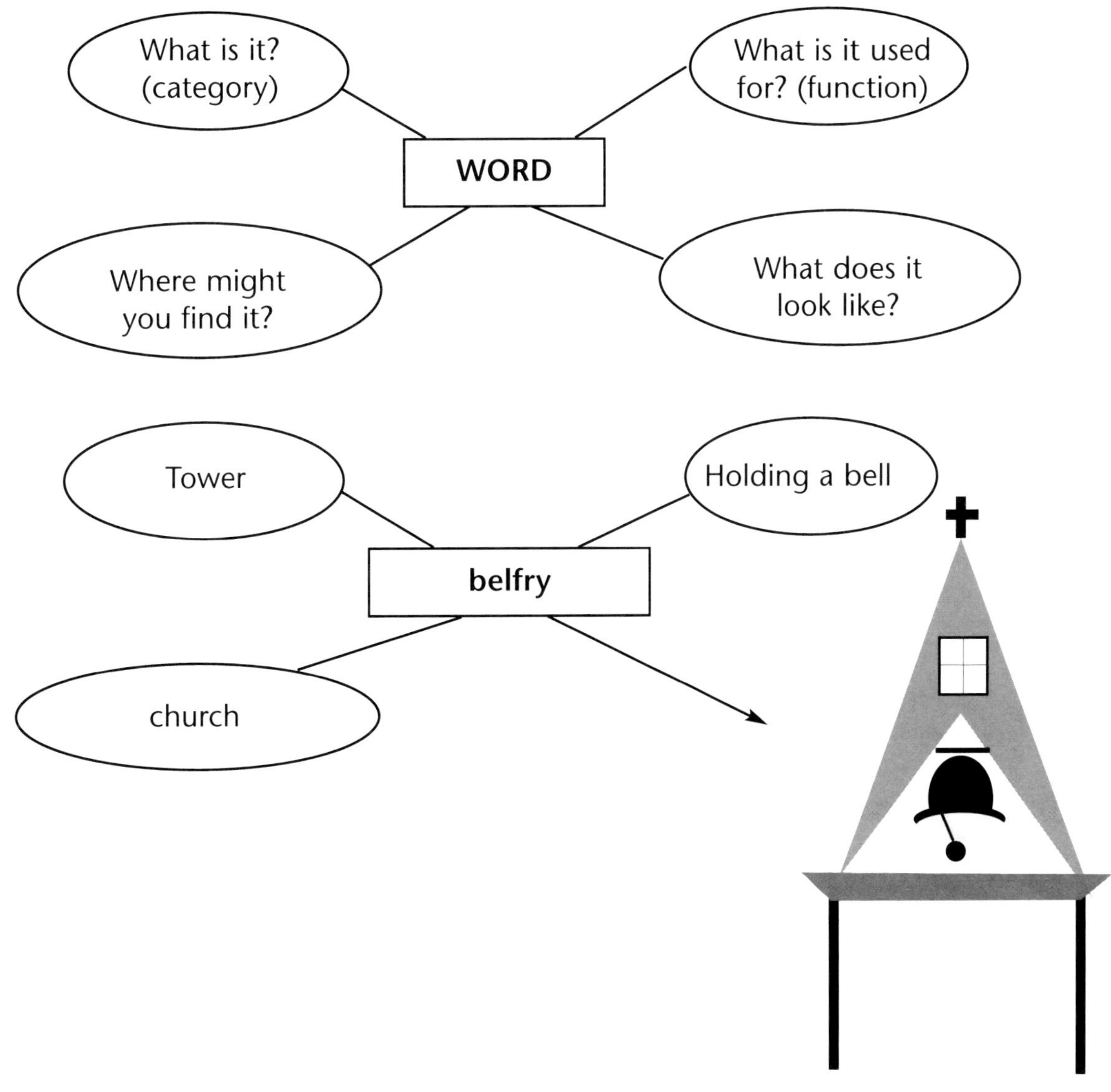

Discussion Questions

1. How successful are Hugh's men? *(Very; The Welsh are completely surprised.)*

2. How is John rewarded for his part in the rescue? *(He is given land and sheep.)*

3. How and when does Robin first see his parents? *(On the afternoon of Christmas Eve, the King and his company—including Robin's parents—arrive in a procession.)*

4. Why doesn't Robin just run to greet his parents? What conflicts does he experience? What would you do? *(He is timid about facing them, but doesn't want to stay in the courtyard and be mistaken for a stableboy.)*

5. How does Peter show his kindness in helping Robin reach a decision? *(He says that he understands Robin's feelings, lets Robin decide what is best for him, and then quickly takes him on his back to the great staircase so that they are both standing, ready to welcome, when the procession arrives.)*

6. How do Robin's parents treat him? *(His mother smothers him with hugs; his father stands back at first, but then embraces him warmly; neither mention the lameness at first—then both say that it doesn't matter.)*

7. Why does the King summon Robin? *(to thank him and give him a jeweled collar—"Sir Robin")*

8. Where will Robin go now? How does he feel at the end? *(He will go with his family back to London after the feast; Brother Luke will be his tutor; he is exhausted, bewildered, happy.)*

Art Activity
Design and inscribe the award the King might give Robin, along with the collar.

Post-reading Questions

1. How does Robin change between the beginning and end of the story? What brings about those changes?

2. In what ways are Robin's problems like those you have? In what ways are they different?

3. What did you learn about medieval times that you didn't know before reading this book? What new questions do you have about that time period?

4. What would you like about living in Robin's time period? What would you dislike?

5. What problems DIDN'T Robin face, which he might have?

6. At what point did you find the story most exciting?

7. How do you think the author went about gathering information before writing this story?

8. Suppose the author had chosen to have the main character be a girl. How would the story have been different?

Post-reading Activities

Suggested Further Readings

1. *The Donkey's Crusade* (Morris)
   Adam of the Road (Gray)
   The Age of Chivalry: English Society 1200-1400 (Wright)
   Anno's Medieval World (Anno)
   Arms and Armor (Byam)
   Arms and Armor (Wilkinson)
   Castle (Macaulay)
   Castles (Smith)
   Cross and Crescent: The Story of the Crusades (Suskind)
   Datelines of World History (Arnold)
   Do You Know? About Castles and Crusaders (Suavain)
   The Encyclopedia of World Costume (Yarwood)
   From Hand to Mouth (Giblin)
   Kings Queens Knights & Jesters: Making Medieval Costumes (Schnurnberger)
   Knights of the Round Table (Gross)
   Learning About: Castles and Palaces (Odor)
   Let's Look at: Castles (Matthews)
   The Luttrell Village: Country Life in the Middle Ages (Sancha)
   Max and Me and the Time Machine (Greer/Ruddick)
   Medieval Days and Ways (Hartman)
   "Medieval Europe," filmstrips with cassettes (Society for Visual Education)
   A Medieval Feast (Aliki)
   A Medieval Monk
   The Middle Ages (Cairns)
   Oars, Sails and Steam: A Picture Book of Ships (Tunis)
   Otto of the Silver Hand (Pyle)
   Pearl in the Egg (Van Woerkom)
   The Pied Piper of Hamelin (Diamond)
   The Reluctant Dragon (Grahame)
   Robin Hood of Sherwood Forest (McGovern)
   Saint George and the Dragon (Hodges)
   The Search for Delicious (Babbit)
   See Inside: A Castle (Unstead)
   See Inside: A Galleon (Rutland)
   The Soldier Through the Ages: The Medieval Knight (Windrow)
   The Story of the Champions of the Round Table (Pyle)
   The Time Traveller Book of Knights and Castles (Hindley)
   What Happened in Hamelin (Skurzynski)
   Wheels: A Pictorial History
   The Whipping Boy (Fleischman) **(Novel Units® guide available)**
   Young People's Story of Our Heritage: The Medieval World (Hillyer/Huey)

Geography

2. Have students locate places mentioned in the story on the map, such as Wales, England-London, and Shropshire.

Art/Bulletin Board Idea

3. With a small group, create a "map" of the journey Robin takes. On a large piece of butcher paper, draw a winding path. Each person then illustrates a scene which occurred at one of the points along the journey (on separate pieces of 8 1/2" x11" paper). The separate illustrations are glued onto the path in the appropriate order, and the small group then adds background illustration to the butcher paper.

Art

4. Using soft wood or soap, try whittling a doll as Robin did. Find arts/crafts books which contain photographs of whittled objects. Make a list of the types of objects people have whittled. (You'll be amazed by the detail and ingenuity whittlers have shown in some of their tiniest creations!)

5. Make a mobile of some of the objects (miniaturized) central to the story, such as the crutch, the doll, the harp.

Music

6. Find recordings of music which might have been heard in Robin's day (e.g., Kyrie's the monks might have sung; music John-go-in-the-Wynd might have played, such as "Love a Garland Is" and "Lament of a Lass").

7. Take the tune of a ballad or folk tune and write new words to it to create a song which tells of Robin's bravery.

Writing

8. Create chapter titles for each of the ten chapters. Remember that a chapter title often refers to a character introduced in that chapter, or a significant event which occurs in that chapter.

9. Write about an "open door" you have found. What problem or obstacle did you face? How did you solve it? Did you recognize the "open door" as a solution, at first?

10. You are Robin, age 20. You now know how to read and write well. Write a letter to Brother Luke. Tell him how you are and what you are doing. Ask him about some of your old friends.

11. Suppose Robin's parents had both died of the plague. Write another ending for the story.

12. Suppose you had been alive in Robin's time. Write a scene in which you meet Robin. Include both dialogue and description.

13. Robin is reunited with his parents at the end. What do you think his thoughts are during those first 10-15 minutes? Write an "interior monologue" which tells those thoughts.

Medieval Feast/Fair

14. Hold your own classroom medieval celebration! Costumes may be as elaborate or simple as you like. Use your imagination in recreating medieval feast-foods (e.g., a boar's head might be fashioned out of hamburger).

Research

15. Find out more about the Newbery Award, which this book won. Do you think the book deserves the award?

16. Look up the entire text from which the title quote was taken (and of which a portion is quoted on the page before the title page). Who is speaking to whom? What do the words mean?

17. Find out more about one of the following topics treated in the story, and create a report in any form you choose (oral report, written report, bulletin board display, diorama, time line, etc.).

    a) the plague
    b) a medieval fair
    c) medieval food
    d) medieval conflicts
    e) medieval pilgrimages
    f) the role of monks in written language
    g) the contrast between the life of a 10-year-old then and now
    h) Oxford University
    i) medieval games still played today (e.g., "hoodman-blind" and "hide-and-seek")
    j) medieval language
    k) medieval clothing
    l) last names and their derivations
    m) medieval calendar of celebrations

Language Study

18. You probably recognize several of the words and expressions used by Robin and the other characters as variants of expressions used today (e.g., "pick-a-back"). Make a list of such expressions in the book. Find out what you can about how the expression started and what it means today. Create a mini-dictionary.

19. Although you can understand what the characters mean, their medieval speech is a little different from modern-day speech. Gather a collection of statements from the book and write modern-day "translations." (e.g., p. 37—"Off with thy jerkin"= "Take off your jacket.")

Activity Sheet: Word Square Puzzle

Directions: Using the clues, put one letter into each box to make a word square. The completed box can be read from top to bottom and from left to right. Example—Clues: medieval boy messenger, melody for a single voice, stringed instrument, action taken on a bell.

H	A	R	P
A	R	I	A
R	I	N	G
P	A	G	E

Clues: 16 letters: John-go-in-the-__________ played a harp; Robin liked to watch birds as they did this in the garden; the Queen wanted Robin's mother to be her __________-in-waiting; the monks may have told Robin stories about this garden in which Adam and Eve resided.

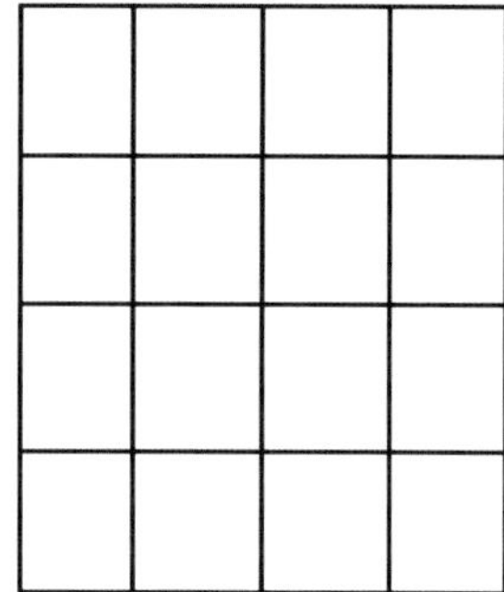

(Answer)

f	*l*	*e*	*w*
l	*a*	*d*	*y*
e	*d*	*e*	*n*
w	*y*	*n*	*d*

Now try making up a 9 or 16-box word square of your own, using 3 or 4 letter words from the story.

Assessment for *The Door in the Wall*

Assessment is an ongoing process. The following ten items can be completed during the novel study. Once finished, the student and teacher will check the work. Points may be added to indicate the level of understanding.

Name ____ Date ____________________

Student   **Teacher**

1. Give yourself one point for each vocabulary activity completed successfully.

2. Write chapter titles that indicate something that might happen or to create suspense to encourage the reader.

3. Complete one of the suggested research projects: organization and function of guilds, Middle Ages, plague, medieval food, medieval conflicts, medieval pilgrimages, medieval clothing.

4. Make an attribute web for one of the characters in the novel.

5. Complete the Decision-Making Chart on page 14.

6. Create a map of the journey Robin takes.

7. Make a mobile of some of the objects (miniaturized) central to the story such as the crutch, the doll, the harp.

8. You are Robin, age 20. You now know how to read and write well. Write a letter to Brother Luke. Tell him how you are and what you are doing. Ask him about some of your old friends.

9. Contribute to a model or mural of the monastery or the castle.

10. What did you learn about the Middle Ages that you did not know before reading this novel? Write three paragraphs to share with classmates and your parents.

Notes

Notes